MATH ATTACK!

Exploring Life Science with Math

EXPLORING DEADLY HABITATS WITH MATH

Robyn Hardyman

PowerKiDS press

New York

Published in 2017 by
The Rosen Publishing Group, Inc.
29 East 21st Street, New York, NY 10010

Cataloging-in-Publication Data
Names: Hardyman, Robyn.
Title: Exploring Deadly Habitats with Math / Robyn Hardyman.
Description: New York : PowerKids Press, 2017. | Series: Math attack: exploring life science with math | Includes index.
Identifiers: ISBN 9781499431216 (pbk.) | ISBN 9781499431230 (library bound) | ISBN 9781499431223 (6 pack)
Subjects: LCSH: Adaptation (Biology)–Juvenile literature. | Extreme environments–Juvenile literature.
Classification: LCC QH546.H349 2017 | DDC 578.4–dc23

Produced for Rosen by Calcium
Editors for Calcium: Sarah Eason and Jennifer Sanderson
Designers for Calcium: Paul Myerscough and Jennie Child
Picture researcher: Rachel Blount

Picture credits: Cover: NOAA: Image courtesy of Expedition to the Deep Slope 2007, NOAA-OE r; Shutterstock: Underworld tl; Inside: NOAA: Image courtesy of Aquapix and Expedition to the Deep Slope 2007 23; Shutterstock: Jose Arcos Aguilar 18, 29t, Jo Crebbin 27, Yasser El Dershaby 26, Cat Downie 6, Matthieu Gallet 6–7t, GybasDigiPhoto 9, HelenField 24, Sebastian Kaulitzki 21, Pavel Krasensky 4, 28t, LauraD 11, Benny Marty 20, Richard A McMillin 22, 29b, NatalieJean 9, 28b, Vladimir Nenezic 19, Khoroshunova Olga 13, Protasov AN 1, Dmytro Pylypenko 8, Nuki Sharir 15t, Stills By Scott 14–15c, Superjoseph 12, Theskaman306 16, Tristan3D 25, Vvvita 5, Brandon Yoshizawa 17.

Manufactured in the United States of America
CPSIA Compliance Information: Batch #BW17PK: For Further Information contact Rosen Publishing, New York, New York at 1-800-237-9932.

CONTENTS

SUPPORTING LIFE

The world is a beautiful place, full of living things. Wherever we look, plants and animals of many different kinds surround us. However, some places are easier to live in than others. A habitat is a place where animals and plants live. The features of a habitat influence the kind of life that can survive there.

Finding Energy

All living things need one basic thing to survive. They need a source of energy. Plants get this from sunlight, which they convert into energy in a process called **photosynthesis**. Animals get their energy from eating food. Herbivores eat only plants. Carnivores eat other animals, including animals that have eaten plants, so even carnivores' energy comes originally from sunlight.

The ants of the Sahara deliberately come out at the hottest time of day to collect the bodies of insects that have died from the heat. Their long legs move quickly over the burning sand.

The Dead Sea is an extreme habitat because it is incredibly salty.

Extreme Habitats

There are some habitats that do not seem to be good homes for most kinds of life. They may be incredibly hot or freezing cold. They may be very dry or very dark. These are known as extreme habitats. The amazing thing is that life does exist in these places. The deserts and the deep sea are full of living things. Some places are even more extreme, yet there is life there, too. Creatures that live in extreme habitats are called extremophiles.

MORE THAN A NUMBER!

THE DEEP OCEAN IS NOT FROZEN BUT IT IS VERY COLD. ABOUT 90 PERCENT OF ALL OCEAN WATER IS AT A TEMPERATURE OF BETWEEN 32° FAHRENHEIT AND 39° FAHRENHEIT (0° C AND 4° C). THAT WOULD FEEL EXTREMELY COLD TO YOU AND ME!

So Hot

The sun beats down on the land, heating it up. A warm, sunny day is usually a pleasure to be out in, but in some places, the sun's heat would be unbearable for most people. Any place where the temperature is regularly more than 100° Fahrenheit (40°C) is called "extreme." There are many habitats that experience these high temperatures. Even there, life has found a way to carry on.

Deserts

A desert is a place that gets less than 10 inches (254 mm) of rain a year. Not all deserts are hot, but some are among the hottest places on Earth. Few plants can grow in a desert, so there is little shade. Still, a few animals can thrive there. Some animals dig holes to stay cool in the day, and come out at night. Others keep their bodies cool by sweating. The fennec fox has special furry paws so it can walk on hot sand.

The fennec fox lives in the Sahara. It digs a den in the sand and keeps cool by losing heat through its very large ears.

The Punchbowl in Yellowstone National Park is a hot spring containing tiny microbes.

Heat from Below

Some habitats are hot because the ground below is heated. For example, in Yellowstone National Park, a huge **supervolcano** lies underground. The heat from the volcano causes hot springs of water to gush out of the ground. The water is too hot for most creatures to live in, but very tiny creatures, called **microbes**, are found there.

MATH ATTACK!

Death Valley in California is the hottest place on Earth and the driest place in North America. The world record for highest air temperature was recorded there in 1913, at 134° Fahrenheit (57° C). About 2 inches (5 cm) of rain falls there every year. How much rain falls in Death Valley over a 55-year period? Use this calculation to help you solve the problem:

2 INCHES X 55 YEARS = ? INCHES

So Cold

The frozen places of the world may seem to be unlikely places for living things to thrive. In the Arctic and the Antarctic, the temperature remains below freezing for most of the year and, in mid-winter, the sun never shines. The Arctic Ocean is covered with sea ice, and in Antarctica, ice covers the land. Still, there is a great variety of plants and animals living in these frozen lands.

The thick layer of fat that leopard seals have below their skin is known as blubber.

The Antarctic

In the Antarctic, there are several **species** of penguins and many other birds, such as the albatross and skua. Penguins have thick layers of fat on their bodies to keep them warm, as well as feathers. The surrounding Southern Ocean is home to whales and seals, and millions of small shrimplike krill.

The Arctic

At the Arctic, around the North Pole, many creatures have found ways to survive. Under the sea ice, Arctic cod swim. They are an important source of food for local birds and **mammals**. Many creatures in this very cold water contain a special substance to keep their blood from freezing. Seals live on the ice, trying to keep away from the polar bears that hunt them. Both have thick layers of fat, called blubber, and fur to keep them warm. The fluffy, white Arctic fox lives in the Arctic, too. In summer, the plants must grow quickly and produce seeds before the winter returns. They grow low to the ground, and the wind spreads their seeds.

Arctic fox

MORE THAN A NUMBER!

IN SUMMER, THE SUN SHINES 24 HOURS A DAY IN THE ARCTIC. THE AVERAGE TEMPERATURE IS 37–54° FAHRENHEIT (3–12° C). IN THE COLDEST WINTER MONTHS, THE SUN NEVER RISES ABOVE THE HORIZON AND EVERYTHING IS IN DARKNESS. THE AVERAGE TEMPERATURE IS -30° FAHRENHEIT (-34° C).

Arctic cottongrass thrives in the short growing season of the Arctic.

EXTREME SALT

Normal ocean water is about 3.5 percent salt. Too much salt is bad for most living things. It makes them dry out and, eventually, it kills them. For some plants and animals, though, extremely salty habitats are their home and they are suited to them.

Great Salt Lake

The Great Salt Lake in Utah is very salty. Its south arm is three to five times saltier than the ocean. Its north arm is even saltier than that. No fish can survive in these parts of the lake, but there are some small animals that can. Saltwater is also known as brine. Millions of brine shrimp live in the lake. They can control how much salt they let into their bodies because their outer layer is waterproof. Brine flies also lay their eggs in the salty waters of the lake. The eggs hatch into **larvae**, which live and feed in the water. Both the shrimp and the flies are important sources of food for birds.

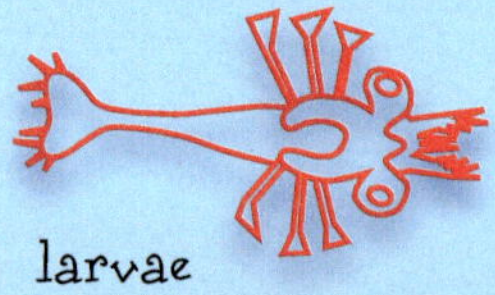

larvae

Plants such as squirrel-tail grass can live in very salty locations on land, such as near the shores of salt lakes.

Seagrasses can live in salty ocean water but not in the super-salty salt lakes.

Salt Lovers

There is one kind of organism, or living thing, that loves a super-salty habitat. It is called a halophile, and it needs salt to live. Halophiles are so tiny they can be seen only with a microscope. Extreme halophiles live in the Dead Sea in the Middle East. The water there contains almost 35 percent salt, making it one of the saltiest bodies of water in the world. At 1,237 feet (377 m) deep, it is also the deepest salt lake in the world.

MATH ATTACK!

Normal ocean water is 3.5 percent salt. The water in the Dead Sea is about 35 percent salt. How much more salty is the Dead Sea than normal ocean water? Use this calculation to help you solve the problem:

35 PERCENT ÷ 3.5 PERCENT = ? TIMES MORE SALTY

Under Pressure

As you travel downward in the ocean or a deep lake, the **pressure** increases and the temperature becomes very cold. There is still some oxygen to support life, though, and some creatures can live there.

Many deep-sea fish have bodies that are mostly water. Their bodies are long and thin, with weak, watery muscles.

Going Down

Humans cannot travel deep under the ocean without protection. Our bodies would be crushed by the high pressure down in the depths. Many other creatures cannot survive there either, but there are some that have adapted to life in this extreme habitat. Our lungs, which are filled with air, are crushed by this pressure. Deep-sea creatures do not have lungs. Instead, they are made up mostly of water, which cannot be crushed. Giant spider crabs also have a protective outer shell for living on the ocean floor 1,000 feet (300 m) down.

Deepest Depths

Way down, it is surprising how many creatures are still swimming around in the cold and dark. Fangtooth fish can live an incredible 16,500 feet (5,000 m) down. Sea lilies look like plants, but they are animals. They can live at depths of about 10,000 feet (3,000 m). They have a stalk that attaches to the seabed, and many feather-like arms that guide food particles into their mouths. Also in the deep are giant shrimplike creatures called amphipods. Unlike most shrimp, these can be more than 1 foot (30 cm) long.

MORE THAN A NUMBER!

HUMANS EXPLORE THE DEPTHS OF THE SEA IN **SUBMERSIBLES**. THESE CAN KEEP THE PRESSURE INSIDE THE VESSEL SAME AS IT IS ON THE OCEAN SURFACE. THE GREATEST DEPTH REACHED BY A SUBMERSIBLE IS 35, 787 FEET (10,908 M), WHICH IS NEARLY THE DEEPEST SPOT ON THE SEABED.

This sea lily is in quite shallow water but they can live thousands of feet below the ocean's surface.

No Water

Places that are very dry can be deadly habitats, too, because living things need water to survive. Dry places are called deserts, and they can be either hot or cold. All deserts receive very little rain. The Atacama Desert in Chile, for example, gets fewer than 0.04 inch (1 mm) of rain a year. That makes it a challenging place for things to live in.

camel

Sahara Challenge

The Sahara in North Africa is the biggest hot desert in the world. It is as large as the United States. Most of it is bare, with dry, scattered rocks or sand. It hardly ever rains there and, during the day, it is incredibly hot. At night, though, it quickly cools down. The animals and plants there make the most of the water that is available. Animals get the water they need from the food they eat. Some have ways of storing it, too. Camels store water in the fat in their humps. They can go without water for a week. Plants store water in their fleshy stems, leaves, or trunks. Their root systems spread over a wide area, to gather up as much water as possible when it does fall.

The giant saguaro cactus is the largest cactus in the United States.

Gentoo penguins live in Antarctica. Unlike most animals, they can drink seawater.

Cold and Dry

Antarctica is the world's biggest desert. The Dry Valleys there are some of the driest places on Earth. Nothing can live there except for some **bacteria**. Elsewhere in Antarctica, though, there is more life. Penguins live on the ice. Although it hardly ever snows, they can get water from the fish they eat. They can also drink salt water.

MATH ATTACK!

The giant saguaro cactus lives in the Sonoran Desert of Arizona. It is adapted for life in the desert. It can grow 50 feet (15 m) tall, and live for up to 200 years. It stores water in its stems and leaves, and can have more than 25 "arms." It grows very slowly. If a saguaro cactus is 10 inches (25 cm) tall and grows 0.5 inch (1.25 cm) per year, how many years will it take to reach 20 inches (50 cm)? Use this calculation to help you solve the problem:

20 INCHES – 10 INCHES = ? INCHES

? INCHES ÷ 0.5 INCH = ? YEARS

No Oxygen

Himalayan yaks are the highest-dwelling animals in the world.

We need oxygen to live. We breathe it in from the air around us, and take it into our lungs. We think of it as essential to all life, but there are some habitats where there is no oxygen. Even there, some forms of life have found a way to live successfully.

The Beginning

When life began on Earth, there was little oxygen in the air. These early forms of life managed without it. That was hundreds of millions of years ago, but the descendants of these life forms are still living. At the bottom of swamps and deep lakes, on the ocean floor, and under huge **glaciers** of ice, there is no oxygen at all. Very basic forms of life such as bacteria live there. Instead of taking in oxygen, they use other **chemicals**, such as iron or sulfur, to create the energy they need to live.

Chinchillas live high up in the Andes Mountains in South America, where the air has less oxygen.

MORE THAN A NUMBER!

THE HIGH-MOUNTAIN HABITAT IS CALLED THE ALPINE BIOME. IT BEGINS AT ABOUT 10,000 FEET (3,000 M) ABOVE SEA LEVEL. IT ENDS AT THE POINT WHERE SNOW COVERS THE GROUND ALL YEAR ROUND. IT IS VERY COLD THERE, TOO. ANIMALS HAVE THICK FUR AND LAYERS OF FAT TO KEEP THEM WARM.

marmot

Way Up High

As the land rises higher above sea level, the air around it changes. At great heights, such as on the tops of mountains, there is much less oxygen in the air. We find it difficult to breathe there without having extra oxygen, but some creatures are suited to this environment. In the Himalayan Mountains in Asia, for example, mammals such as the marmot, the snow leopard, and the yak, can live as high up as 17,000 feet (5,200 m) or more. They have bigger lungs and hearts than other animals to make the most of the oxygen available to them.

ALTERED BY HUMANS

In many parts of the world, the ways in which we live have affected the habitats of animals and plants. We have torn down forests, plowed up land to grow crops, and built towns and cities on huge areas of open country. Our search for **raw materials** has also affected habitats. Many places where animals and plants used to live successfully have become much more difficult for them to live in.

In this river, chemicals have fed algae. The algae have formed a blanket over the surface. Other forms of life in the river die out as a result.

Pollution

Industries often produce harmful substances that are released into the environment. This is called pollution. Chemicals may run into streams or soak into the earth. In water, they kill fish and plants. In the ground, they may be taken up by plants, and then eaten by animals, which are then harmed or killed. Farming can damage natural habitats. Many farmers use chemicals on their crops to help them grow and kill pests, and these run into streams and rivers. They then kill fish, birds, and insects.

Mining

Mining for coal or metals can impact habitats that are far away from the mine. It can add large quantities of soil and rock to rivers. These build up and make the river slow down or change course. Chemicals from mines also poison the water. Habitats are often destroyed to create the mine. Sometimes, our activities are just too loud for the creatures of the natural world. In the Arctic, the noise of oil and gas exploration is so loud that some kinds of whale have difficulty feeding and breeding.

This open coal-mining pit has destroyed a large area of habitat that plants and animals once enjoyed.

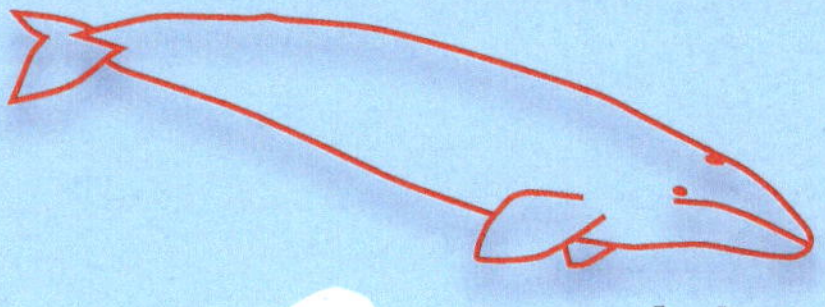

whale

MATH ATTACK!

Imagine 500 different species live in every 10 square miles (26 square km) of land. If 30 square miles (78 square km) of land are totally cleared for a mine, how many different species lose their habitat? Use this calculation to help you solve the problem:

30 SQUARE MILES ÷ 10 SQUARE MILES = ?

? X 500 SPECIES = ? SPECIES

ACIDS AND RADIATION

Even without human action, some places on Earth are naturally extremely harsh. Conditions there make it difficult for all but the most extreme creatures to live.

The microbes living in this hot spring in Yellowstone National Park give the spring its vibrant colors.

Acids and Bases

Acids and **bases** are two kinds of chemicals. A scale called the pH scale measures how acidic or basic a substance is. A low pH number means the substance is very acidic. A high pH number means it is very basic. Strong acids will burn our skin and are harmful to most living things. Some habitats are naturally very acidic, such as hot springs. These bubble up from underground, heated by the rock below. Even there, tiny microbes live and reproduce. The different species give the water different colors.

Radiation

Radiation is an invisible kind of energy that is given off by substances that are unstable. This means they are constantly breaking down. Radiation is dangerous to humans, and to most living things, because it causes changes in our bodies that can make us sick. Some habitats naturally have higher levels of radiation than normal. Caves and other places underground can have **radioactive** materials, but microbes can successfully live there, too.

MORE THAN A NUMBER!

TARDIGRADES ARE TINY ANIMALS THAT CAN LIVE IN HIGH PRESSURE, HIGH AND LOW TEMPERATURES, AND RADIATION. THEY CAN SURVIVE 1,000 TIMES MORE RADIATION THAN WOULD KILL A HUMAN BEING, AND LOW TEMPERATURES OF -454° FAHRENHEIT (-270° C).

Tardigrades are the absolute champion survivors of extreme habitats. They have even survived being in space.

So Dark

No light can reach deep down in the ocean, yet in this extreme habitat, many creatures are living. They have special features that allow them to survive in the inky darkness.

See for Yourself

In a place where there is no light, it makes sense for creatures to provide their own. This is exactly what anglerfish do. They have a long spine on their backs with a glowing tip. They wave this about in the water to attract their prey. Lanternfish go one step farther. They can light up all along their underside, tail, and head. This ability of animals to produce light is called bioluminescence. Many creatures of the deep ocean have very large eyes, to catch any glimmers of light there might be. The vampire squid has the largest eyes relative to its body size of any animal. It uses its eight arms to feel its way in the dark.

This moon jellyfish has a soft, glowing bioluminescence.

Giant Tube Worms

At the very bottom of the Pacific Ocean it is completely dark, but giant tube worms live in the boiling water that spews out of **hydrothermal vents**. These are cracks in the rock that have let in water. The water is heated by very hot rocks below and comes gushing back up. What is more, this boiling water is full of chemicals that most living things would find poisonous. The giant tube worms feed off bacteria in these chemicals to make their energy. They grow up to 8 feet (2.4 m) long, and have bright-red parts on one end for feeding.

Giant tube worms live in the ocean at about 5,000 feet (1,500 m) deep.

MATH ATTACK!

If a diving vessel sinks down through the dark waters of the ocean by 100 feet (30 m) every 10 minutes, how many hours will it take the vessel to sink 3,000 feet (915 m)? An hour has 60 minutes. Use this calculation to help you solve the problem:

3,000 FEET ÷ 100 FEET = ?

? X 10 MINUTES = ? MINUTES

? MINUTES ÷ 60 MINUTES = ? HOURS

When Earth Was Young

Earth

If we could travel back billions of years to when Earth was young, we would see that most of its environments on it were extreme. There was not much oxygen, and the first simple life forms were developing in a soupy liquid. Scientists are very interested to study the extreme habitats of the world today because they may contain clues to a much bigger picture.

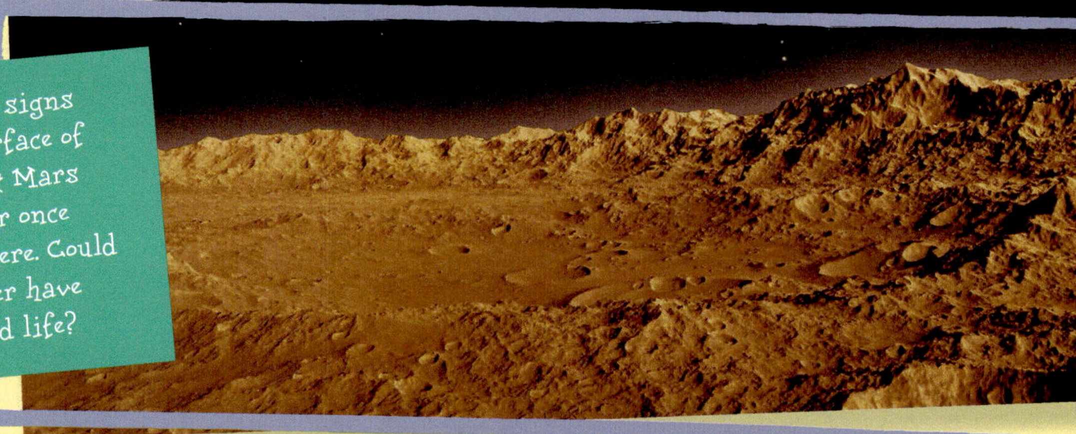

There are signs on the surface of the planet Mars that water once flowed there. Could that water have contained life?

Life Beginning

Studying life in extreme habitats helps us learn more about the history of life on our planet. Over millions of years, simple, tiny organisms that could make their own food using the energy of the sun, eventually developed into plants. Plants create oxygen during photosynthesis, and oxygen is what most animals need to breathe to survive. So without these amazing early creatures, animals would not have developed, and life on our planet would not be as we know it today.

Europa is one of the moons of the planet Jupiter. Could there be an ocean below its icy surface, and could it contain life?

MORE THAN A NUMBER!

THE SURFACE OF EUROPA, ONE OF JUPITER'S MOONS, IS COVERED IN ICE SEVERAL MILES THICK. BENEATH THE ICE THERE MAY BE AN OCEAN CONTAINING TWICE AS MUCH WATER AS THERE IS ON EARTH. EUROPA IS 600 MILLION MILES (966 MILLION KM) AWAY, SO TO REACH IT WILL TAKE AT LEAST 6 YEARS.

Other Planets

Understanding these extreme life forms also gives us an amazing chance to learn about the possibility of life on other planets. We know that other planets have extreme environments. They can be very dry, hot, or cold. They can be acidic, without oxygen, and high in radiation. Could it be that they are home to similar kinds of life as we have found on Earth? The methods and instruments used to explore these habitats on Earth can be used to test other planets, too. Scientists tested the instruments sent to explore the surface of Mars in the dry Atacama Desert of Chile.

DESIGNED FOR SURVIVAL

We have seen that many places on Earth seem very unlikely habitats for animals and plants. They are extremely cold or hot; they have no water or no light. They have dangerous levels of radiation or of acids. Yet, life has found a way to survive there.

Perfectly Adapted

As long as plants and animals can find a source of food to give them energy, they can live. They develop **adaptations** to suit the places where they live. Warm fur and fat provide heat in cold places. Water-storing features aid survival in the desert for both animals and plants. In the darkest places, some animals can even create their own light through bioluminescence. Even in the saltiest and most acidic places, microbes of many colors have found a way to survive.

These camels are perfectly adapted for life in the hot, dry desert.

Even habitats that seem extreme are full of life.

What Can We Learn?

This incredible variety and ability of living things to adapt teaches us some important lessons. It shows us that we should never assume that life is impossible in any environment. We should explore everywhere, to discover the secrets of the natural world. It also shows that we cannot always know what effect our actions are having on our planet. We should take care not to destroy any habitat, however extreme it may seem, because there is almost certain to be something living there.

MATH ATTACK!

If scientists exploring the extreme habitat of another planet found 40 life-forms every week of their study, how many life-forms would they find if their study lasted for 30 weeks? Use this calculation to help you solve the problem:

40 LIFE-FORMS X 30 WEEKS = ? LIFE-FORMS

ANSWERS

Now that you have read many facts and figures about deadly habitats, try to learn more. It would be good to find out where your nearest challenging habitat is.

Here are the answers to the Math Attack problems. How did you score?

PAGE 7:

2 INCHES X 55 YEARS
= 110 INCHES

PAGE 11:

35 PERCENT ÷ 3.5 PERCENT
= 10 TIMES MORE SALTY

PAGE 15:

20 INCHES – 10 INCHES = 10 INCHES

10 INCHES ÷ 0.5 INCH = 20 YEARS

PAGE 19:

30 SQUARE MILES
÷ 10 SQUARE MILES = 3

3 X 500 SPECIES = 1,500 SPECIES

PAGE 23:

3,000 FEET ÷ 100 FEET = 30

30 X 10 MINUTES = 300 MINUTES

300 MINUTES ÷ 60 MINUTES = 5 HOURS

PAGE 27:

40 LIFE-FORMS X 30 WEEKS
= 1,200 LIFE-FORMS

GLOSSARY

acids Substances that have a pH less than 7.

adaptations Features of an animal's body, or of its behavior, that help it survive.

bacteria Tiny organisms.

bases Substances that have a pH greater than 7.

chemicals Substances made by a chemical process, either by humans or naturally.

glaciers Large, solid masses of ice in a mountain valley.

horizon Where the sky and land appear to meet.

hydrothermal vents Cracks in the seafloor, through which hot water spurts.

larvae The stage in the life of an insect after it hatches from an egg.

mammals Animals that give birth to live young and feed them with milk.

microbes Incredibly small organisms that are invisible to the naked eye.

photosynthesis The process plants use to make their food from the energy in sunlight.

pressure Pushing force.

radioactive Having or producing a powerful and dangerous form of energy, called radiation.

raw materials Natural substances used in industry.

species A kind of living thing.

submersibles Vessels that can travel under the sea.

supervolcano A very big volcano under the ground.

FURTHER READING

Books

Animal Planet and L. Brown. *Polar Animals (Animal Bites)*. New York, NY: Liberty Street, 2016.

Jenkins, S. *The Animal Book*. Boston, MA: HMH Books for Young Readers, 2013.

Ringstad, Arnold. *Forest Habitats*. Mankato, MN : Child's World, 2014.

Rizzo, J. *Ocean Animals: Who's Who in the Deep Blue*. Washington, DC: National Geographic, 2016.

Websites

Due to the changing nature of Internet links, PowerKids Press has developed an online list of websites related to the subject of this book. This site is updated regularly. Please use this link to access the list:
www.powerkidslinks.com/ma/habitats

INDEX